Original title:
The Rhymes of Red Cedar

Copyright © 2025 Creative Arts Management OÜ
All rights reserved.

Author: Liam Sterling
ISBN HARDBACK: 978-1-80567-322-4
ISBN PAPERBACK: 978-1-80567-621-8

Scent of the Cedar Breeze

In the forest, trees do prance,
Cedar scents to make you dance.
Squirrels wear their acorn hats,
Birds sing tunes like chubby cats.

Oh, the breeze brings giggles near,
Rustling leaves with joyful cheer.
Come and smell the perfume strong,
In this woods, you can't go wrong.

A Treetop Serenade

High above, the branches sway,
Cedar wood has much to say.
Chirping birds forget the time,
Their silly songs, a jumbled rhyme.

A raccoon strums on old tree bark,
Playing tunes that hit the mark.
How the squirrels love to groove,
In this treetop, they get to move.

Secrets Nestled in the Bark

In the crevices, secrets hide,
Whispering tales of joy and pride.
A woodpecker taps a peppy beat,
While ants parade on tiny feet.

Cedar whispers, 'Join the fun!'
As dusk sets in, the day is done.
Chasing shadows, making friends,
In this grove, the laughter blends.

Dance of the Rustic Winds

When the wind begins to twirl,
Cedar branches sway and whirl.
With every gust, a tickle here,
Leaves giggle, spreading cheer.

Oh, the dance, it never ends,
Nature's jesters, all our friends.
With a spin, and a leap, and a whiff,
Cedar laughs, oh what a gift!

Cedar Perception

A tree stood tall with a crooked grin,
Pine cones bouncing like kids in a spin.
It whispered jokes to the passing breeze,
While squirrels chuckled, dropping their keys.

Its bark held secrets of laughter and strife,
Tales of the forest, oh what a life!
Branches waving as if to say,
"Come join my party, let's dance and play!"

The Canvas of Green

In the meadow where colors collide,
A painter with leaves took the green side.
He dipped his brush in the dew of the morn,
Creating a masterpiece—nature reborn!

With splashes of laughter across the sky,
Bees buzzed along, creating a high.
"Look at my work!" the wind did proclaim,
"Cedar's the name, fun's my middle name!"

Tones of the Natural World

A concert of critters in the bright light,
Creaky old branches put up a fight.
A chorus of birds sang out loud and clear,
While the frogs croaked jokes to everyone near.

The sunset giggled, painted pink skies,
Even the clouds wore balloon-like ties.
"Nature's a stage," said the wise old tree,
"Come laugh and join this grand jubilee!"

Fables of the Forest's Heart

Once in a glen where the laughter is free,
Lived a wise old cedar who spoke to a bee.
"Tell me a tale from the lands up high!"
The bee buzzed softly, "I'll try not to cry!"

"Once I was huge, but oh what a fright!
A kid threw a rock and I shrank overnight.
Now I'm a legend in stories from far,
With these tiny adventures, I'm now a star!"

Harmonies of Sap and Soil

In a forest of giggles, the trees dress in green,
The sap sings a tune, quite a funny scene.
Roots perform salsa, while branches do waltz,
Nature's own comedy, with no hints of faults.

A squirrel in a top hat, conducts with a smile,
While mushrooms break dance, each move full of style.
The bark cracks a joke, and the saplings all giggle,
As leaves fall for laughter, and the branches all wriggle.

The Patter of Autumn Leaves

Leaves whisper secrets in the crisp autumn air,
Each flutter a chuckle, without a single care.
They tumble and twirl, like jesters in flight,
A parade of the funny, in colors so bright.

Acorns huddle close, sharing tales of delight,
Of squirrels who tripped in the morning light.
With a rustle and shuffle, the forest joins in,
As laughter from nature, is the real win!

The Flora's Embrace

A daisy once dated a sprightly old weed,
Their romance was funny, but just what they need.
They danced through the garden, arms all entwined,
While bees buzzed a tune, completely maligned.

The roses wore sneakers, they ran for the fun,
While daisies all laughed, saying, 'Look at us run!'
In this botanical bash, every bloom plays a part,
Where petals and laughter just bloom from the heart.

Memory of Roots

Deep in the soil, where the stories are kept,
Roots reminisce with a chuckle, sidestepped.
They gossip of storms and the rain that once fell,
Each tale grows more silly, as they laugh and they swell.

Old tree trunks recall, with a wink and a nudge,
The time that a squirrel made a very wrong fudge.
From their underground meetings, comes a giggly cheer,
For every root's memory brings laughter near!

Amongst the Whispering Pines

In the woods where squirrels dance,
Frogs practice their hopping stance.
Trees giggle with a creaky sound,
While acorns tumble to the ground.

A rabbit wore a tiny hat,
Said, "I'm stylish, just like that!"
The owls laugh with wise old eyes,
As mice throw cheese for party pies.

Heritage of the Woodland Breeze

The breeze comes in with ticklish glee,
It plays pranks on the bumblebee.
Leaves flutter like they just might sing,
As raccoons plan their masquerading.

A hedgehog trips on a fallen twig,
Spins around, does a little jig!
From every bush, a joke is told,
Nature's laughter never gets old.

The Cedar's Chronicle

Once a cedar rapped its bark,
Hosting tales that hit the mark.
It spoke of stars that played charades,
And critters lost in evening parades.

A fox with flair and a sly little grin,
Danced like nobody's watching him.
The entire glade began to cheer,
Echoing laughter, loud and clear.

Flickers of a Sunlit Glade

In a sunbeam's merry light,
Daisies giggle with delight.
Butterflies in costumes bright,
Flap their wings, what a sight!

A gopher plays a game of peek,
Poking his head from his little creek.
Dancing shadows sway and sway,
Making mischief all the day.

The Lure of the Quiet Woods

In the woods where squirrels dance,
The trees wear jackets, not a chance.
A raccoon in a top hat struts,
While owls gossip in funny huts.

The crickets chirp a wacky tune,
As frogs in shades hop 'neath the moon.
The breeze tells jokes to rustling leaves,
In laughter woven through the eaves.

A deer with glasses reads a book,
While pinecones drop with clever looks.
The pines chuckle, tickle their roots,
As chipmunks trade their tiny suits.

So if you're seeking a silly thrill,
Head to the woods for a hearty fill.
Where nature's antics steal the show,
And the humor in the greenery flows.

Canvas of the Old Pine

Old pine stands tall, a painter's muse,
With squirrels debating the best views.
Bark like canvas, a twist of fate,
Hosting a gallery in nature's state.

Bumblebees buzzing, loud and proud,
In the gallery of branches, they form a crowd.
A raccoon artist with paint-stained paws,
Creates abstract art without a pause.

With pine needles as brushes, they swirl,
As ladybugs dance and twirl and twirl.
A canvas of greens, with sunshine spritz,
Each creature adds their quirky bits.

In this funny world wrapped in trees,
Laughter lingers in the gentle breeze.
Where art is nature's playful spree,
And pines chuckle at their creativity.

Echoes of Timber and Time

In the forest where trees go boom,
Squirrels dance in a leafy room.
The branches chuckle with every sway,
Woodpeckers laugh at the break of day.

Mice wear boots just to glide on leaves,
While raccoons play hide and seek with thieves.
A bear does cartwheels, oh what a sight!
Nature's circus in the soft moonlight.

The logs gossip about the winds,
Sharing tales of their woodland sins.
When the rain comes, they all take cover,
But the puddles call them for a playful hover.

So if you wander where woodlands thrive,
Keep your ears open, feel alive.
Each whisper's a jingle, a raucous tune,
Nature's a comedian under the moon.

The Rustle of Resilient Roots

Roots rumble like a well-told joke,
Tickling each pebble, it's no hoax.
Down below, they dance in glee,
While branches sway, "Come and see!"

Ants set up a café in the shade,
Serving acorn lattes, homemade.
Bees are the baristas, just so spry,
Buzzing in rhythm, like they can fly.

The moss throws a party, all things green,
Fungi arrive, look at them glean!
Each mushroom sports a tiny hat,
While frog DJs spin—imagine that!

So wander near roots that twist and bend,
Where laughter and whimsy seem to blend.
Underneath, all those little sights,
Nature's comedy unfolds, full of lights.

Trails of Red in the Twilight

Beneath the twilight, treetops sway,
Whispers of red, come join the play.
Signposts pointing to a chipmunk's stash,
Promising snacks, oh what a bash!

The sun dips low, and shadows creep,
But squirrels chatter, not one is steeped.
Acorns roll like marbles in a game,
While owls hoot, "You'll never tame!"

Berries laugh on the branches high,
Chasing each other as they fly.
Rabbits hop in a conga line,
It's a twilight party, mighty fine.

So trail the red, let giggles ring,
Where critters are kings and dance with zing.
Under the stars, that's where you'll see,
Nature's delight in unity.

Memories Wrapped in Arbor

Branches whisper secrets of days gone past,
Reminders of laughter that forever last.
Wind chimes giggle, how they sway,
As sunlight dips in a playful ballet.

Bark tells stories, rough with age,
Like a comedian, it's on the stage.
Each knot and groove holds a tale to spin,
Of daring snoozes and cheeky grins.

Leaves flutter down like confetti bright,
A celebration of nature's delight.
Chipmunks toast with acorn cheers,
Old tree trunks laugh, shedding years.

So linger beneath the boughs so wide,
Where memories hug you, side by side.
In the embrace of the timber's charm,
Life unfolds with a twist, warm and calm.

Ancestry of the Knotted Roots

In a forest where cousins converge,
Knots in their trunks start to emerge.
Branches gossip of old family trees,
Aunt Maple heckles with a teasing breeze.

With roots intertwined, they laugh and spin,
Old Grandpa Oak boasts of his win.
Sister Spruce thinks she's the best-dressed one,
While Brother Pine claims the tallest run.

Their trunks entwined in a tangled dance,
Mother Nature giggles at the chance.
Every ring a laugh from years gone by,
In this leafy house, the fun is spry.

The Wisping Breeze

A whisper of wind tickles the trees,
It plays hide and seek, just to tease.
Round and round, it takes a spin,
Even the squirrels join in with a grin.

The chatter in leaves, a giggly sight,
As branches sway to the breeze's delight.
"Catch me if you can!" the wind will shout,
While the birds chirp loudly, "What's that about?"

The clouds join in, they puffy-laugh,
Drawing silly faces, a comical craft.
In this woodland play, all creatures agree,
Fun lives in every rustling spree!

Celestial Cedar Whispers

Stars peek through branches, taking a chance,
To listen in on a tree's lively dance.
"Tell us a story!" the moon shines bright,
While firs whisper tales in the shimmering night.

A pine with a grin shares a joke or two,
The cosmos chuckles, as if it knew.
"Why did the twig break? It was under a limb!"
"Oh come on!" the stars cry, "That's over the brim!"

With every soft rustle, the laughter grows,
Echoing tales that nobody knows.
Nature's own jesters, under dark skies,
Knotted in humor where the laughter flies!

Skylines Framed in Green

Up high in the clouds, the trees take a stand,
Framing the skyline with nature's hand.
"Look at us, stylish, with hats of leaves!"
The branches flirt, as summer grieves.

The city beneath sings a mundane tune,
While trees wear their crowns and dance with the moon.
"Let's start a trend!" whispers a bold birch,
"Who needs a runway? We'll own our own perch!"

Swaying in chorus, they cheer and sway,
Mocking the traffic, come join the ballet!
With laughter and green, they uplift the scene,
Creating a skyline that's quite a marine.

Guardians of the Forest Floor

Beneath the boughs where squirrels play,
The forest's floor is a buffet.
Mushrooms dance in their earthy shoes,
While ants proclaim, "We've got the blues!"

A rabbit sneezes, the leaves all shake,
The chipmunks giggle, their tails awake.
With every step, a crunch, a knick,
Oh dear, what's this? A dancing stick!

The rocks are laughing, the trees eavesdrop,
It's hard to tell when the giggles stop.
Each creature here has a joke to tell,
In the forest floor, all's funny as a bell!

So next time you wander, take care to listen,
To the whispers of nature; oh, how they glisten!
We're all just jesters in this grand show,
Where laughter abounds, and the wild things glow.

Nestled in the Habitat

In cozy nooks where feathers fluff,
Birds gossip 'bout their latest stuff.
A raccoon thinks he's quite the chap,
While deer just roll their eyes and nap.

"Is that a snack or just a prank?"
The creatures wonder, "What's the rank?"
A badger smirks and eats a sprout,
"Oh come now friends, let's play it out!"

The pond reflects a loafing frog,
Who dreams of being a sturdy log.
The turtles chuckle and take their bets,
On which of them gets the most new sets!

In this habitat, absurdity thrives,
Where every creature's humor survives.
So, dear friend, if you ever pass through,
Remember, laughter's the best kind of glue!

The Whispering of the Timbers

The trees start whispering tales so tall,
Of lumberjacks who tripped and fell.
'Wouldn't it hurt if you did that twice?'
They cackle and sway, oh isn't it nice?

A woodpecker knocks, 'Hey, who's there?'
"Just the trees joking, no need to fear!"
The owls hoot, "We've heard that one before,
But let's hear it again, just to make sure!"

Branches bend low, they lean and tease,
"Who'd wrap up tight in the summer breeze?"
A squirrel drops acorns, one bounces high,
"Catch me if you can!" he dares, oh my!

So listen close to the timbered tongues,
Their whispers dance like a chorus sung.
A forest filled with giggles and glee,
Where every crack and creak sets humor free!

Interpretations of the Natural World

In every nook, a tale unfolds,
Interpretations, funny and bold.
A fox paints pictures with its quick paws,
While a hedgehog dreams up some lofty laws.

A flower cries, "What a sight I bloom!"
While bees hold court in their buzzing room.
The grass tickles rabbits, "Dance a jig!"
And the ants march on, all quite big!

The clouds float by, wearing silly hats,
While shadows play games with curious cats.
Each leaf has seen some fun-filled days,
With parades of critters in crazy ways!

Nature's canvas, painted so bright,
With laughter sprinkled, what a delight!
So explore the world, let giggles unfurl,
In this funny realm, life's a whirl!

Whispers of the Whispering Boughs

In the forest where shadows play,
A squirrel steals snacks by the bay.
The trees gossip with a chuckle,
About the acorns and the buckle.

Boughs leaning low, they tease the breeze,
Telling tales with teasing ease.
A spider spins a web of sighs,
As birds debate their fashion ties.

Laughter dances in the air,
A woodpecker joins without a care.
Together, they echo nature's laugh,
In this grand, green photograph.

Cedar whispers, secrets shared,
With every gust, we're all ensnared.
Here in the woods, life's never bland,
Just a wacky, wild band of land.

Echoes Beneath the Canopy

Underneath the leafy dome,
Creatures scurry, finding home.
A chipmunk makes a silly face,
A beetle joins in the race.

Branches shake with hearts so light,
As owls crack jokes throughout the night.
"Why did the rabbit cross the road?"
"Oh dear, ask a toad!" they goad.

Cedar needles drop like rain,
Tickling toes in this playful game.
Roots weave stories bold and bright,
Beneath the stars, they ignite the night.

Every sound a giggle, every rustle cheer,
The forest is full of funny here.
Whispers turn to roars of glee,
In this wild, leafy jubilee!

The Secrets of Scarlet Wood

In the depths of scarlet dreams,
A raccoon plots with sneaky schemes.
Stealing berries, oh what fun,
Underneath the golden sun.

The bushes chuckle at his quest,
As whispers thread from nest to nest.
"Watch out!" shout the squirrels, so spry,
"Don't get caught! Just say goodbye!"

Every branch a joker's grin,
As laughter weaves the woodland din.
A jester deer trots through the wood,
With antics that are all too good.

Cedar sings of mischief here,
Echoing joy, never fear.
In this vibrant, lively nook,
Laughter's found in every crook.

Tapestry of Rustling Needles

In the glades where sunbeams bounce,
Ants gorge on crumbs, they slyly pounce.
A tiny frog claims royal crown,
Croaking jokes while he hops around.

The needles flutter, share a jest,
"Why sit still when you can rest?"
Crickets wink with rhythmic strum,
Join in the giggles, oh how they hum!

Trees sway softly, plotting their tricks,
As branches dance in twirling kicks.
A puppy barks, a playtime scene,
As shadows flicker, bright and keen.

Rustling tales through twilight hours,
Nature's laughter, wild and ours.
In this garland of giggles found,
Life's vibrant stitches weave around.

A Ballad of Bark and Breeze

The bark was thick, the jokes quite slick,
A cedar tree with sass did speak.
Its branches swayed, a merry dance,
While squirrels laughed, and took a chance.

With birds that chirped in silly tones,
They spun around, like dancing drones.
The sun peeked in, with a cheeky grin,
While shadows played, and giggles spun.

Old roots told tales of squirrels' feats,
Of acorn heists and nutty cheats.
The breeze was light, a friendly tease,
Inviting all for laughter's ease.

Now every knock upon its wood,
Rang out like laughter, pure and good.
In nature's crowd, the fun's on deck,
Among the branches, we lose all check.

Where Time Stands Tall

In a world where the minutes crawl,
The cedar claims it stands so tall.
It tick-tocks slow, with leaves that sway,
Making time take a playful play.

A chipmunk stopped to joke with bees,
Who buzzed along with perfect ease.
While shadows stretched, the sun did race,
Crowned by laughter, a funny face.

Each knot a story, each branch a cheer,
With every glance, the fun drew near.
Tickled trunks and giggly vines,
In this green realm, where joy entwines.

So if you stroll beneath this crown,
Don't frown, nor let your smile drown.
For in its shade, life takes a break,
And time will dance, for laughter's sake.

Underneath the Cedar Sky

Underneath a canopy so wise,
Laughter echoes, hopes do rise.
The whispers tickle, the leaves applaud,
As humor blooms on path well-trod.

A rabbit hopped with funky flair,
While squirrels played, without a care.
The sunshine sparkled, laughter flew,
In every breeze, a joke that grew.

The world around spun wild and bright,
Beneath the boughs, all feels just right.
Each child's giggle a melody,
A joyous tune 'neath cedar's tree.

So come and frolic, bring your cheer,
For life is grand when friends are near.
In this funny glade, let's make our play,
Where joy and laughter seize the day.

Nature's Lullaby of Resilience

In nature's cradle, jokes abound,
Where every laugh is nature's sound.
Cedar stands with strength and grace,
A bastion of smiles in every space.

With storms that roar and winds that tease,
It bends and sways, still dons a breeze.
The creatures chirp, with wit so bright,
Turning troubles into pure delight.

Rain may fall and clouds parade,
Yet underneath, there's no charade.
For every setback brings a grin,
Resilience lives where fun begins.

So lean on bark and take a seat,
Join in the fun, feel the heartbeat.
For the laughter sung by tree and sky,
Is nature's lullaby, oh my oh my!

The Song of the Cedar Groves

In a grove where trees meet,
The squirrels dance with glee.
A chipmunk in his tux,
Claims he's the star, you see!

The branches sway and twist,
As birds crack jokes on high.
A crow shouts, 'You missed!'
While the owl just rolls his eye.

The breeze begins to hum,
As leaves join in the song.
With notes of sweet perfume,
It won't be long, not long!

So gather 'round, dear friends,
In this merry old place.
Where laughter never ends,
And every tree has grace.

Nature's Timeless Verse

The pinecones drop like bombs,
As squirrels commence their war.
The logs form tiny homes,
While bugs prepare a tour.

A deer slips on a stone,
And lands with quite a thud.
The rabbits look amazed,
'Good job, you silly bud!'

The winds play peek-a-boo,
With shades of green and brown.
A cicada sings a tune,
That makes the leaves dance 'round.

So raise a twig or two,
And cheer for nature's fun!
In every shade and hue,
The laughter's just begun!

Cedars in the Mist

Through the fog, a whisper calls,
As misty Cedars blend.
A raccoon in a shawl,
Claims to be a forest friend.

The shadows creep and slide,
As critters play their tricks.
A shadow on the side,
Cries out, 'Don't take those sticks!'

The branches softly sway,
A giggle in the breeze.
The owls join in the fray,
While rabbits aim to tease.

So let's enjoy the laugh,
When the mist begins to clear.
Nature loves a good photograph,
With friends, it holds so dear!

Harmony of the Forest Floor

On the floor where twigs do snap,
The ants throw quite a ball.
A slug slips in a nap,
While crickets sing and crawl.

With mushrooms dressed in spots,
Like party hats, so neat.
The caterpillar trots,
On tiny wobbly feet.

A raccoon steals a snack,
While badgers play at catch.
The trees, they form a pack,
To watch this wild fetch match!

So if you hear the sound,
Of laughter in the air.
It's nature's joy unbound,
With friends who truly care!

Poetry in the Grain

In a forest where whispers giggle,
Trees dance around, oh what a wiggle!
Squirrels recite their acorn tales,
While owls hoot jokes on breezy trails.

Branches nod, they're quite the jesters,
Bringing laughter like true investors.
Mice tap-dance on treetop beats,
While beetles groove in tiny feats.

Saplings shrug, with much disdain,
Complaining 'bout the weather's drain.
Even roots get in on the fun,
Tickling earth 'til the day is done.

In this wood, with quips so spry,
Nature's laughter lifts us high!
So grab a seat beneath the green,
And join the show, it's quite the scene!

Shadows Cast by Ancient Giants

Tall trunks stretch to tickle skies,
Casting shadows, oh my, surprise!
Raccoons plan their midnight plots,
While frogs croak votes with silly thoughts.

With bark like laughter, trees take a stand,
Having meetings, oh isn't it grand?
Branches wave, a frisky group,
While pine cones gossip, sharing the scoop.

Sunbeams peek with a fidgety grin,
As squirrels debate who's going to win.
With playful nudges, the limbs embrace,
A comedy show in nature's space.

In these shadows, hilarity sways,
As giants chuckle through their days.
A kingdom of quirks where giggles sprout,
Nature's humor is what it's all about!

A Heartbeat in the Evergreen

In a grove where whispers bloom,
Laughter echoes, chasing gloom.
Birds chirp jokes, what a delightful scene,
As butterflies twirl in a sparkling sheen.

Cedar branches sway in the breeze,
Tickling noses, oh, what a tease!
The ground is alive with the softest sigh,
While crickets perform, oh my, oh my!

Pine needles drop like silly confetti,
Creating a carpet, oh so ready.
Beneath the boughs, a bear takes a nap,
Dreaming of honey and a cozy trap.

With every gust, a chuckle unfolds,
Nature tells tales in whispers bold.
So in this encore of leafy cheer,
Join in the fun, no need to fear!

Life Among the Aromatic Pines

Pines stand tall, with scents divine,
While squirrels skit in a comedic line.
They tumble down, then strike a pose,
While bees buzz gossip, everyone knows!

The air is thick with playful taunts,
As moles trade stories with drama fronts.
Dewdrops giggle on morning grass,
As sunflower heads bob, oh what a class!

Whispers of pine create a song,
A harmony where we all belong.
Even the rocks have something to say,
Joking about who'll trip on the way.

So let's wander through this whimsical scene,
With trees and creatures in vibrant sheen.
Life's a jest, let laughter align,
In nature's embrace among the pines!

The Cedar's Silent Watch

Under the stars, the cedar stands tall,
Whispers of secrets it keeps for us all.
Squirrels debate over acorn delight,
While owls hoot softly, 'It's party night!'

With branches so wide, it offers a seat,
For raccoons and owls who just want to meet.
They share funny tales of the creatures below,
In a language only the trees seem to know.

The wind it does tickle the bark with a tease,
As pinecones drop down, 'Oh, do mind your knees!'
Who knew a tree could make us all giggle,
With each little rustle and every small wiggle?

And as the moon grins, it plays peek-a-boo,
Oh, what a scene when the skies turn blue!
The cedar just chuckles, a heart full of cheer,
Keeping the laughter of nature so near.

Tales from the Timber Trails

Amidst the tall pines, the critters convene,
With stories so wild, you know what I mean!
A fox once got lost, chasing its tail,
While bees buzz around with a sweet, buzzy wail.

The chipmunks have gossip, oh dear, that's a sin,
Trading their stories, they cackle and spin.
A deer ran away from a mischievous hare,
Both laughing it off with the sun in their hair.

The pathways of timber are paved with delight,
As the raccoons retell all their daring night fights.
While frogs croak their verses, a melodic refrain,
In the great comedy of nature, no one's ever plain.

So fill up your laughter, it's free to receive,
The timber will echo whatever you believe.
Let's dance with the shadows, play silly, be bright,
In the tales of the timber, we unwind with good light.

Nature's Rustic Lullaby

In the heart of the woods, where the wild things hum,
A lullaby sings with a twang and a drum.
The pine needles rustle, a tickle for ears,
As crickets assist in composing the cheers.

The old log sits grinning, with moss as its hat,
While raccoons are plotting their next little spat.
The owls are the chorus, they sleepily croon,
'Turn down the volume, or we'll miss the moon!'

Around the campfire, where stories ignite,
A bear tells a joke, and the fireflies light.
With giggles spreading like sap on a tree,
Laughter flows wild, a contagious decree.

The brook joins in, with a giggle and splash,
As the frogs leap high in a silly, slimy dash.
So here in the woods, with the stars up above,
Nature whispers sweetly, a lullaby of love.

Pollen and Pine

In the garden of green, the pollen does dance,
While bees wear their buzz like a bright, silly prance.
They sip and they flutter, not missing a beat,
As the flowers all chuckle, 'Ain't life so sweet?'

With a sneeze and a wheeze, the wind goes 'achoo!'
Each flower laughs softly, 'What now is to do?'
'Don't mind that big bear, he's just here for tea,'
While the butterflies giggle, 'Oh, just let it be!'

As pine needles fall, like confetti from trees,
The squirrels throw parties, with acorns as keys.
They waltz on the branches, in sync and in time,
Creating their own little silly mime rhyme.

So join in the fun, let your laughter soar high,
In a world where the trees are the stars of the sky.
Pollen and pine, a whimsical mix,
Nature's own punchline, with all of its tricks.

Twilight's Embrace on Cedar Loam

In twilight's grip, the trees conspire,
With whispers low that spark desire.
A squirrel winks, a bird will jest,
As daylight fades, they seek their rest.

A fox with flair, he struts about,
Telling tales with a cheerful shout.
The moonlight dances, sassy and spry,
While shadows giggle, passing by.

Roots entwined like friends at play,
They mold the ground in a comical way.
Cedar branches sway with glee,
As crickets chirp their symphony.

The night unfolds, a merry show,
As stars appear, all in a row.
With laughter rich and voices loud,
Nature thrives, so fun, so proud.

Guardians of the Green

Amidst the leaves, a gnome stands tall,
His cap askew, just short of a fall.
He guards the shrubs with a wink and a grin,
Blessing the blooms, let the mischief begin!

A raccoon rambles, searching for snacks,
His tiny paws, no time to relax.
Chasing shadows, he leaps with flair,
While crickets whistle without a care.

Wise old owls, with glasses askew,
Debate the night's news in a hoot or two.
The elder tree chuckles, creaking so loud,
As fireflies flicker, they gather a crowd.

Together they plot under night's grand dome,
In this woodland kingdom, they all feel home.
With laughter and cheer, friends big and small,
Guardians of green, they welcome us all.

Redwood Reveries

Tall as the tales that they wrapped around,
Redwoods stand sturdy, roots in the ground.
With knots like smiles, they share their dreams,
As squirrels plot mischief, or so it seems.

A chipmunk's dance, it's a sight to see,
He spins and twirls, as happy as can be.
Falls into acorns, the mound is a mess,
Yet he simply chuckles—it's all for the jest.

Dewdrops shine, like giggles afloat,
While raccoons wear masks for a friendly vote.
In a world of whimsy, nothing goes wrong,
In the heart of the wood, they all sing a song.

As shadows grow long, they've had their fun,
With stories of joy, the night's just begun.
Under the stars, they all come together,
Redwoods and friends in fine, funny weather.

Hues of the Woodland Soul

Colors collide where the wild things play,
A tapestry woven in playful display.
Yellow and purple, with green in the mix,
Nature's palette paints joy with her tricks.

A jester jay perches high on a limb,
With a squawk and a flap, he starts on a whim.
He hops down low and spins in surprise,
While a curious hedgehog peeks with wide eyes.

The earthworms giggle beneath leafy shrouds,
Telling tall tales of the passing clouds.
In vibrant hues, they shimmy and sway,
As the sun dips low, ending the day.

With joy in each leaf and laughs all around,
The woodland soul in every sight and sound.
In shades so bright, we find our delight,
In the hues of the forest, everything's right.

A Tapestry Woven in Green

In the forest where squirrels play,
Cedar trees twist and sway.
A beaver in shades of gray,
Constructs his home with flair each day.

Pinecones fall like comical hats,
Dancing clumsily as they chat.
The raccoon tries to make a spat,
While woefully missing where he's at.

A woodpecker taps to the beat,
While ants parade on tiny feet.
A party in shades so sweet,
With nature's rhythm, none can beat.

With laughter woven through each scene,
All coexist in vibrant green.
Underneath the tall, serene,
Life's a festival, so fun and keen.

Twilight Serenades

As dusk unfolds its velvet cloak,
The fireflies begin to poke.
A frog sings out with every croak,
While raccoons plan their little joke.

The owls hoot in silly tones,
While crickets play their silly phones.
Up above, a tired bird moans,
Dreaming of chairs made of cone stones.

Chasing shadows, the night owls roam,
Searching for snacks in their tree home.
With giggles echoing, they comb,
Through twilight, making mischief foam.

In the twilight cast in pastel light,
Creatures dance with sheer delight.
Each serenade feels just right,
As they celebrate the night.

Woodcraft Whispers

In the glade where wood meets air,
Crafty creatures work with flair.
A squirrel's nutty art affair,
Has everyone else stop and stare.

A crafty beaver starts to build,
His dams with laughter easily filled.
The goose nearby is less than thrilled,
At all the havoc nature's spilled.

A woodchuck chuckles from his nook,
Inspired by stories and a good book.
With tools made from nature, he took,
To create a masterpiece with every hook.

Under the cedar's watchful eyes,
Mischief brews with every surprise.
When woodcraft seems to arise,
Nature giggles; oh how time flies!

Cedar Dreams at Dusk

Underneath the cedar's boughs,
Creatures gather, singing vows.
A party starts, with little cows,
Dancing wildly, oh, what a rouse!

Firelight flickers, shadows prance,
A raccoon leads the woeful dance.
With every misstep, they take a chance,
Giggles erupt with this wild romance.

As stars peek in with a glimmering grin,
Dreams of mischief are sure to begin.
Laughter swells, like warm apple skin,
In the company of friends, all is win.

At dusk, when silence starts to creep,
The merry band remains in a heap.
Stories shared, and secrets to keep,
Oh, cedar dreams, how fun it is to leap!

Vignettes of the Verdant Realm

In the woods a squirrel prances,
Dancing as it takes its chances.
It flips and flops, a sight to see,
Stealing acorns, wild and free.

Underneath a tree so tall,
A raccoon prepares to brawl.
With a cat, it stirs up chaos,
Over leftovers, like a play-cast!

Birds chirp tunes that crack us up,
One tries to land, just spills its cup.
Diving straight and missing trees,
Rubbing dreams off of a breeze.

The leaves giggle in the breeze,
Whispering jokes with such ease.
In this green, comical realm,
Nature wears its fun crown, a helm.

Seasons Shared with Tall Sentinels

Spring brings blossoms, oh so bright,
Bees buzzing, oh what a sight!
A bunny hops, with a wink and twitch,
Stealing carrots—what a glitch!

Summer sun, the kids run wild,
Splashing in puddles, joy of a child.
A bear in shades, cooling in the creek,
Who invited him to the picnic peak?

Fall brings crunch beneath our feet,
Pumpkin spice makes life a treat.
A raccoon with a scarf clashes,
In search of food, through leaves he dashes.

Winter blankets with silver snow,
Snowmen formed, with carrot nose glow.
A penguin wanders, sees a hat,
Waddles off, we laugh at that!

The Sage of Scented Shadows

In the shade, a wise old tree,
Whispers secrets, come hear me!
A fox debates—it's a strange tête-à-tête,
On who can jump the fence, a bet!

A skunk strolls by with style and flair,
Leaves a trail—oh, we beware!
Yet all the critters seem to cheer,
"Who wore it best?!" is the atmosphere.

Twirling leaves in shadow games,
Casting shapes, with funny names.
A beetle acts as if it's grand,
Dancing disco, quite the band!

Echoed giggles from squirrel to owl,
The sage chuckles, "What a row!"
In the scented shadows, laughter lingers,
With each funny twist, we point our fingers.

Connections in the Wooded Heart

In the heart of green, friends unite,
From leaf to leaf, the joke takes flight.
A deer cracks puns, a real charmer,
While a tortoise shares tales of farmer!

The butterflies laugh, flitting about,
"Who's the funniest?" they tease and shout.
A bear chimes in with a lively roar,
"Tell me more, I'm always up for more!"

The shadows dance with glee and mirth,
While the critters sing their egg-cellent worth.
"All together now, let's raise a toast,
To friendship and giggles, we love the most!"

As dusk falls, the laughter's sweet,
Echoing through each cozy street.
In the wooded heart, joy shines bright,
In every corner, humor takes flight.

Cedar Symphony

In the forest, giants sway,
Their needles tickle, come what may.
A squirrel dance, a chipmunk's cheer,
In this concert, loud and clear.

With acorns falling, plop, plop, plop,
The treefolk gather, hop, hop, hop.
They sing of rain and shadowed cheer,
And giggle at the passing deer.

Branches jive to nature's beat,
As raccoons tap with tiny feet.
The woodpecker drums, a quirky sound,
These cedar jams, there's joy abound!

The twilight comes, the stars peep in,
The forest band will soon begin.
With laughter echoing through the wood,
Everyone leaves feeling good!

A Harmony of Needle and Bark

Cedar trees wear hats of green,
In the sunlight, a dazzling sheen.
They gossip softly with the breeze,
Sharing secrets, laughing with ease.

The squirrels host a nutty show,
While owls mingle, wearing their glow.
Each branch a stage, each leaf a fan,
For every creature in the clan.

Woodpeckers tapping, what a noise,
Joining in, those lively boys.
With every peck, a rhythm made,
Under the green, a grand parade!

As moonlight spills on tree and ground,
All the funny tales abound.
In cedar canopies up high,
The forest tales will never die!

Treetop Tales

Above the world, where laughter roams,
The cedars sing of far-off homes.
With each gust, a twist of fate,
A funny breeze, they sway and prate.

A crow brings news, a joke or two,
The chipmunks chuckle, "What's that, who?"
A dance-off starts, the branches shake,
As nature's jesters play and wake.

Frogs leap high in hush-hush glee,
"Let's do the twist!" they croak with glee.
In treetop realms, such joys abound,
With silly sounds, the woods resound.

As daytime wanes and shadows play,
Cedar friends laugh the night away.
In every nook, a giggle hides,
In happy heartwood, joy abides!

Constellations of Cedar Dreams

At dusk, the twinkling stars appear,
The tree tops frame what's crystal clear.
A raccoon points out a funny shape,
"Is that a dream or just a grape?"

With laughter, the owls hoot a tune,
The moon joins in, a silver boon.
The needles stand like tiny flags,
Waving stories of moose and snags.

A dancing frog leaps high with flair,
While fireflies glow, as if to dare.
The cedar tales stretch far and wide,
With giggles wrapped in forest pride.

In dreams where cedar spirits weave,
All creatures join, they jump and cleave.
Under the stars, they spin and beam,
In the forest's heart, all share a dream!

Singing with Squirrels

Squirrels chatter high and low,
Chasing tails in a lively show.
They hold a concert in the trees,
While I laugh at their silly tease.

Nutty notes fly through the air,
One drops their snack without a care.
A chorus led by fluffy tails,
In nature's stage, no room for fails.

Dance of leaves, a joyful tune,
Squirrels twirl beneath the moon.
Their acorn hats, a fashion sight,
A nutty bash, what pure delight!

Branches sway with every jump,
Squirrels land with a playful thump.
In the woods, no dullness found,
Just furry fun, and laughter's sound.

Portrait of an Old Growth

A tree so wise with tales to tell,
It stands so tall, tastes like caramel.
Knotted bark and branches wide,
It whispers secrets from inside.

A squirrel's den and a bird's parade,
A gallery where art's displayed.
The knots and bends, a quirky style,
The tree just laughs, 'I've stood awhile!'

Fungi hats and mossy shoes,
Its epic face, a rowdy muse.
Nature's canvas, painted green,
An old-growth chuckle heard unseen.

Roots that stretch wide, stories untold,
In every ring, the years unfold.
With a wink, it shakes its leaves,
At the busy world, it chuckles and weaves.

Beneath the Sweeping Canopy

Underneath a leafy dome,
The squirrels wiggle, call it home.
A tapestry of green and brown,
Where laughter's echoed all around.

The shadows dance as branches sway,
Squirrels host a nutty ballet.
They giggle and leap with grace refined,
Beneath the canopy, joy's entwined.

Cracks and creaks add to the song,
As the tree hums, it can't be wrong.
"Where's my nut?" cries a curious chap,
In this leafy hall, they take a nap.

Sunbeams peek through gaps above,
Every rustle is a word of love.
Beneath this roof, they play all day,
Creating smiles in a funny way.

Stories Carved in the Grain

Each groove a tale, each line a laugh,
Nature's script in a wooden path.
A sneaky chipmunk leaves its mark,
Drawing circles in the bark.

With every ring, a birthday cheer,
Grains whisper "Party's happening here!"
Tree trunks chuckle as they grow,
Sharing wisdom, don't you know?

Woodpeckers drum in rhythm's beat,
Playing tunes that can't be beat.
The squirrels jump, a lively crew,
They claim the stage, and time's their view.

Carved with stories, hoots, and grins,
The laughter blends, and life begins.
In every grain, a jolly tale,
Nature's jesters, they prevail.

Underneath Verdant Wings

Beneath the green, a squirrel sings,
Chasing dreams on bouncy springs.
He trips on leaves with a comic flair,
While birds roll laughter through the air.

A woodpecker taps a silly beat,
As raccoons waltz on tiny feet.
The sunbeams dance, a playful tease,
While ants in suits march with great ease.

Trees whisper secrets, strange but fine,
Of owls who plot for extra time.
With hats and capes, the critters play,
In this forest, joy holds sway.

So join the fun, come take a peek,
Where laughter's found, no word's too weak.
The tales we weave in leafy glee,
Bring smiles to all, just wait and see.

Heartstrings of Forest Lore

In a glade where stories bloom,
A chipmunk plans a grand costume.
With acorn crowns and threads of pine,
He spins a tale that's simply divine.

A rabbit hops, with mischief fraught,
In socks too large, he trips and caught.
The owls hoot with laughter bright,
While crickets chirp to the silly night.

Each tree holds tales of giddy strife,
Of beetles playing pranks on life.
Together, we'll craft this forest fun,
With giggles shared 'til day is done.

So gather round, let's spin and weave,
A symphony of joy, we believe.
In every nook, let laughter soar,
In heartstrings tied to forest lore.

Flickering Candles of the Woods

As fireflies light the night, oh dear,
A bear tries dancing, filling us with cheer.
He wobbles and rocks, then takes a fall,
While frogs croak tunes, the best of all.

Beneath the trees, a jolly band,
Plays spoons and tambourines so grand.
The foxes clap, their rhythm tight,
As stars twinkle with pure delight.

A hedgehog strums a leafy tune,
While raccoons chase the glowing moon.
With colors bright, the night unfolds,
In this woodland, joy never grows old.

So grab a partner, let's make some noise,
With laughter strong, we'll share our joys.
In flickering candles, we find our place,
In nature's dance and warm embrace.

Emblems in the Canopy

Up in the trees, a parade we see,
With monkeys swinging playfully.
A squirrel in shades strikes a pose,
While laughter bursts like blooming rose.

The owls wear ties, so debonair,
As creatures gather, without a care.
The raccoon chef mixes up a feast,
With berry pies, he's quite the beast!

A snail accidentally slides on by,
With a hat too big, he waves goodbye.
While underfoot, the mushrooms grin,
As forest friends tune in for fun to begin.

In canopy high, with laughter loud,
Nature's stage, a merry crowd.
So let's embrace this joyous spree,
In every branch, our souls fly free.

The Call of Nature's Heart

In the forest's embrace I dance,
With squirrels who think they can prance.
They chatter and jump with such flair,
While I wonder if life's just a dare.

The trees sway and giggle, it's true,
As I trip in my old, muddy shoe.
A raccoon looks up and just grins,
As I tumble down, showing my sins.

Birds join the laughter, oh what a sight,
They tease with their songs, what a delight!
I wave at the branches, I barely can stand,
Nature's a riot, oh isn't it grand?

With each step, I find joy in the mess,
In the foliage green, I feel truly blessed.
And though nature's wild, with its comedic twist,
I'll follow the call, 'cause how could I resist?

An Ode to Verdant Giants

Oh mighty trees, with branches so wide,
You tickle the sky as you stand with pride.
You wear coats of green, so splendid and bright,
While birds choose your shoulders for their morning flight.

Chanting the tales of the winds that blow,
As I pray to avoid what the squirrels know.
Those cheeky little nuts, with their grand acorn stash,
I just hope they don't hold an acorn bash!

Your roots are like secrets, hidden away,
But whispering laughter in a magical way.
With each passing season, you sport a new dress,
From blossoms to needles, you never digress.

So here's to the giants, the wise and the grand,
With a tickle of sunshine and a soft helping hand.
In your leafy laughter, I find my delight,
Dancing in shadows, till the fall of the night.

Cradled in Nature's Arms

In the cradle of leaves, I lay down to rest,
While bees buzz along, feeling truly blessed.
A nap in the sun sounds like pure delight,
Until a woodpecker's peck makes me take flight!

The breeze whispers secrets, it's quite a charmer,
Yet tickling my nose like a playful farmer.
I sneeze, and the dandelions burst into glee,
As butterflies laugh, dancing wild and free!

Oh, the wonders of this whimsical place,
With deer who are prancing like they're in a race.
I join in the fun, with a skip and a hop,
Till I trip on a root and go down with a plop!

But nature just giggles, it's hard to stay mad,
Every moment outdoors turns the grumpy to glad.
In the arms of green giants, I find pure cheer,
Through laughter and nature, I'm lost and I'm free here.

Cedar Stanzas

Oh, cedars that tower, so tall and grand,
You tickle the clouds with your noble hand.
You swish and sway, like dancers in tune,
While I fumble my way, singing out of tune.

The critters below hold the grandest of shows,
With raccoons as jesters in whimsical clothes.
They laugh at my trips, while I wave and I grin,
Nature's big circus, let the fun begin!

The sunlight spills laughter, each golden ray,
Creating a stage for my mischievous play.
I tumble and giggle, lost in the scene,
In the arms of the cedars, I'm truly a queen!

So here's to the moments, to silliness found,
In the heart of the woods, with a soft, squishy ground.
With each giggle and tumble, I dance to the beat,
In a world full of laughter, I feel so complete.

Dances in the Dappled Light

Sunbeams waltz on the forest floor,
Squirrels spinning, what a score!
Leaves giggle in a breezy jest,
Nature's party—who needs rest?

Mice tap dance on tiny toes,
While owls squawk in grandiose shows.
Breezes tickle, giggles roar,
In the glade, we all explore!

Frogs croak out a silly tune,
Dancing underneath a glowing moon.
With every leap, they thump and play,
A froggy ballet, hooray, hooray!

Twinkling stars join in delight,
As fireflies buzz, illuminating night.
Nature's humor, pure and bright,
Oh, what fun, what pure delight!

Fragments of Summer's Embrace

Picnics planned by shady trees,
Ants join in to steal your cheese!
Silly hats and lemonade,
Summer laughter, memories made!

Butterflies flap with flashy flair,
Bees buzzing, a wild affair.
A sunburned nose, oh what a sight,
We laugh till it's dark, pure delight!

Kites fly high, caught on a twig,
A tale of woe, just like a gig.
Bubbles floating, kids in a chase,
Chasing laughter—what a race!

Summer's warmth, a friendly tease,
Nature joins the fun with ease.
Each moment held with tight embrace,
In the sun's glow, our happy place!

Whispers of the Ancient Wood

Trees gossip about the breeze,
Raccoons chuckle with great ease.
Mossy blankets, comfy spots,
Cozy corners where laughter's caught!

Woodpeckers tap, a rhythmic beat,
As chipmunks scamper on tiny feet.
The ancient wood, full of glee,
Nature's laughter, wild and free!

Squirrels wear their acorn crowns,
While shadows dance in leafy gowns.
Echoes of joy, a nature tune,
Underneath the watchful moon!

Branches sway in playful jest,
Nature's comedy, simply the best.
With every rustle, a giggle shared,
In the woodland, all is spared!

Echoes in the Canopy

Up above, the branches sway,
A monkey swinging, "Let's play today!"
Parrots squawk their silly songs,
In this realm, nothing feels wrong!

Dizzy vines twist and twine,
As critters shout, "Oh, that's just fine!"
Laughter echoes through the trees,
Whispers carried by the breeze.

Clouds drift lazily, a fluffy crew,
While lizards lounge, enjoying the view.
Every rustle and cackle taps,
Nature's comedy of giggles and laughs!

In this jungle, wild and bright,
Every day's a silly fright.
Echoes bounce with gleeful cheer,
In the canopy, fun is near!

Whispers of Wind in the Woodlands

In the forest, a squirrel plays,
With acorns stashed in funny ways.
A breeze tickles the leaves,
And everyone just heaves.

A crow caws in hilarious tones,
As he hops around on old stones.
The wind sings a quirky tune,
While the rabbits dance under the moon.

Mice gather to share their cheese,
Telling tales with the greatest ease.
Each story a whimsical treat,
In the laughter, they find their beat.

Even the trees shake with glee,
As the wind swirls around with glee.
In the thicket, it's quite absurd,
The chattering of each little bird.

Sketches of Serenity

On a branch, a snoring bat,
Dreams of being a fancy cat.
Pillow of leaves, soft and green,
A humorous sight, seldom seen.

A turtle trots, with wobbly zest,
Knowing well he's never the best.
Slow and steady, he takes a leap,
Laughing at friends who're fast asleep.

The pond ripples with giggling frogs,
Jumping around like silly dogs.
They croak out jokes, ribbit and croon,
Turning the calm into a cartoon.

In the stillness, a breeze plays tricks,
Making the flowers dance with flicks.
What a scene of sweet delight,
Nature's comedy, pure and bright.

The Soliloquy of Saplings

A young sapling in playful chat,
Wonders why it's not a cat.
"Can I climb like a vine?" it asks,
While sunlight plays in playful masks.

Leaves shake with laughter's delight,
As the sapling dreams of flight.
A breeze carries funny tales,
Of mischief in enchanted trails.

Roots giggle beneath the ground,
As they listen to echoes abound.
"Why can't we sway like the trees?"
They chant their requests with ease.

Nearby, a squirrel starts to jest,
"Stop dreaming and give it a rest!"
With smiles and chuckles all around,
In sapling jokes, joy is found.

Memory Lanes of Rough Bark

Rough bark is layered with age,
Tales of jokes on every page.
Knots and grooves tell of the past,
Where giggles linger and always last.

A wise owl hoots with disdain,
"It's not too easy being plain!"
As he spins yarns of fallen leaves,
Dancing stories the old tree weaves.

Beneath, a badger rolls in glee,
Covered in mud so carefree.
Hilarity marks his every slide,
In laughter's warmth, he takes pride.

As dusk arrives, noise starts to fade,
Echoes of mirth in the glade.
A soft chuckle rings in the bark,
Memory lanes dance till it's dark.

www.ingramcontent.com/pod-product-compliance
Lightning Source LLC
Chambersburg PA
CBHW071838160426
43209CB00003B/334